A SURVIVOR'S RECOLLECTIONS OF

THE WHITMAN MASSACRE

MATILDA J. SAGER DELANEY

1920

Contents

MATILDA DELANEY

Even had she not had the sad history of being the survivor of one of the most famous attacks by Native-Americans on civilians, Matilda Jane Sager Delaney's life was one of great interest to anyone interested in westward expansion and the pioneers of the American west.

Matilda was only a child when her parents emigrated to the west. Her father and mother both died on the trail on the way. The Whitmans took the orphaned children in at their mission and cared for them for three years. Matilda witnessed the killing of her brother and others during the attack on Whitman mission.

In 1855, at the tender age of sixteen, Matilda was married for the first time, which she describes below, to Lewis Mackey Hazlett. He died of cancer in June of 1863, leaving her with five children. In 1866, she married her husband's partner, Matthew Fultz with whom she moved to Farmington, Washington, where they ran a hotel and several other businesses. They were married for 18 years when Fultz died in 1884. Six years later, Matilda married David Delaney (1828–1905). At some point prior to his death, they moved to Spokane.

By 1910, Matilda was living with her married daughter, Mattie Hye, in Spokane, Washington. She died in Reseda, California in 1928. The headstone of her second husband in Farmington includes her name.

FOREWORD

The thought of fostering care seems to have remained with this "survivor" since her days with the Whitmans.

Forgiving innocent ones for the atrocious acts of their kindred upon her own brothers, Mrs. Delaney became a benefactor of the Indians. Before the apportionment of their lands the Coeur d'Alene squaws and children suffered great hardships. To them the Farmington Hotel kitchen was a haven of warmth and plenty. They started home cheered and fed with bundles of food to tie on their ponies. The Delaney living room is the only place I have seen Indian women and girls light hearted and chatty. They loved to linger to sing for their hostess. Mrs. Delaney's hospitality extended to clergymen of all creeds. Hers has been a life of hard but generous service. "Not to be ministered unto but to minister" seems to have been the life motto of this woman reared in the wilds.

In 1881 General and Mrs. T. R. Tannatt came to the Northwest when the latter began a search for historical data; she sought pioneers and recorded their statements for comparison, in an effort to obtain truth. Opportunity gave her acquaintance with Mr. Gray, author of History of Oregon, Rev. Cushing Eels, the Spalding family, several survivors of the Whitman massacre, and pioneer army and railway officers from whom she gleaned information which later assisted her in writing the booklet, *Indian Battles of the Inland Empire in 1858*, published by the D. A. R.

In 1887 she stopped at the Farmington hotel owned by Mrs. Delaney, and continued an acquaintance with her until 1920. She said Mrs. Delaney's account of the massacre never varied, and in discussion of points of difference with other survivors Mrs. Delaney's clear description and logical reasoning invariably convinced the others that she must be correct, while her clear remembrance of subsequent events, known to them both for more than three decades, strengthened Mrs. Tannatt's belief in the accuracy of her earlier impressions.

Mrs. Tannatt often urged this witness of the heartrending tragedy to publish her recollections, and had the pleasure of reading the manuscript for this narrative which she said contained the most comprehensive and truthful description of the Whitman massacre she had seen. She consented to write the Foreword, but before doing so was summoned by her Heavenly Father.

MIRIAM TANNATT MERRIAM

PRELUDE TO THE MASSACRE

In the spring of 1844 we started to make the journey across the plains with ox teams. I was born in 1839, October 16th, near St. Joseph, Mo., which was a very small town on the extreme frontier, right on the Missouri River, with just a few houses. My father's name was Henry Sager. He moved from Virginia to Ohio, then to Indiana and from there to Missouri. My mother's name was Naomi Camey-Sager. In the month of April, 1844, my father got the Oregon fever and we started west for the Oregon Territory. Our teams were oxen and for the start we went to Independence, the rendezvous where the companies were made up to come across the plains. There were six children then—one was born on the journey, making seven in all.

The men of the company organized in a military manner, having their captain and other officers, for they were going through the Indian country and guards had to be put out for the protection of the travelers and to herd the stock. The immigration of '43 was piloted through by Dr. Whitman and ours was the second immigration across the mountains. The road was only a trail and was all Indian territory at that time, from the Missouri River to the Rocky Mountains. We had to ferry streams, sometimes with canoes fastened together and the wagons put on them; and the Indians rowed us across the rivers in some places. The mountains were steep and sometimes we had to unyoke our cattle and drive them down, letting the wagons down by ropes. The Captain of our company was named William Shaw. There were vast herds of buffalo on the plains and wandering bands of Indians. We had to guard the cattle at night by taking turns. After we started across the plains we traveled slowly; and one day in getting out of the wagon my oldest sister caught her dress and her leg was broken by the wheel running over it. There was no doctor in our company, but there was a German doctor by the name of Dagan in the following company and he and my father fixed up the leg and from that time on the old doctor stayed with us and helped. My father was taken sick with the mountain fever and he finally died and was buried on the banks of the Green River in Wyoming. His last request was that Captain

Shaw take charge of us and see us safe through to the Whitman station. He thought that was as far as we could go that winter. Twenty-six days later my mother died. She made the same request of Captain Shaw and called us around her and told my brothers to always stay with us and keep us together—meaning the girls of the family. Dr. Dagan came on and helped to care for us with the boys' help. When my mother died, my injured sister could walk only with the help of a crutch. Mother was wrapped in a blanket and buried by the side of the road. So the Captain and his wife looked after us and the other immigrants showed their concern for the orphans by taking an interest in us. A kind woman, Mrs. Eads, took the tiny baby and the big-hearted travelers shared their last piece of bread with us. We finally arrived at Dr. Whitman's station on the 17th day of October, 1844, seven months from the Missouri River to the Whitman station. It was a long time!

Mrs. Whitman wanted to keep the girls, but she did not care for the boys. Dr. Dagan went on the Willamette valley and left us there. Doctor Whitman finally concluded he would keep the whole seven of us and took us in charge. We lived there three years. I might say something of the home incidents. The first thing Mrs. Whitman did was to cut our hair, wash and scrub us, as we were very much in need of a cleaning up; then she gave us something to eat and the bread seemed very dark to us—it was unbolted flour. Mrs. Eads, who had been caring for my baby sister, five months old, arrived three days later and then Mrs. Whitman took the motherless little one in charge and she grew to be a fine baby. Everything was so different from what we had been used to. The Whitmans were New England people and we were taken into their home and they began the routine of teaching and disciplining us in the old Puritan way of raising and training children—very different to the way of the plains. They hired a teacher and the immigrant families all had the privilege of sending their children to this school during the winter months. We had a church and Sunday school every Sabbath and we had our family worship every morning and evening. We had certain things to do at a certain hour. We never had anything but corn meal mush and milk for our suppers and they were very particular in our being very regular in all our habits of eating and sleeping.

5

When the spring came all the immigrants left and went on down to the Willamette valley—the families who had wintered at the Mission leaving the Sager children behind with the big-hearted Dr. and Mrs. Whitman. We had our different kinds of work to do. We had to plant all the gardens and raise vegetables for the immigrants who came in for supplies. We got up early in the morning and we each had our piece of garden to weed and tend. We had to wipe the dishes and mop the floors. We had verses of scripture to learn each morning which we had to repeat at the family worship. The seven verses would be our Sunday school lesson. We took turns in giving our passages of Scripture. Everything was done in routine. Sometimes we had to walk in the afternoon. Mrs. Whitman would go with us; we would gather specimens and she would teach us botany. During the summer when the Indians went to the buffalo grounds, we were alone and we looked forward to the coming of the immigrants as one of the great events of our life. Sometimes in the summer we went bathing in the river. We would get the Indian girls to teach us to swim. Once, Missionary and Mrs. Eels came down from Walker's Prairie, having with them a girl by the name of Emma Hobson, and the latter went in bathing with us children; she could not swim and the current swept her down the river. She caught on an overhanging bush and an Indian took her out of the river and put a blanket around her. Mrs. Eels gave the alarm. We always called that "Emma's place." We cut water melons in two and strung them together and would play for hours with those water melon boats, having a great deal of enjoyment. Still, discipline was strict and when we were told to do a thing, no matter what, we went.

Once a month we had a missionary meeting and we would sing missionary hymns and the Whitmans would read extracts from missionary papers. They took the Sandwich Island paper, the editor being the Rev. Damon. There was a man at the Mission by the name of O'Kelley; he was an Irishman, and he went with the Doctor who had to go out and give the Indians a lesson in farming. They took all we girls in a wagon and this man O'Kelley drove. Dr. Whitman showed the Indians how to cultivate their little patches. There was not very much cultivation about anything, however. O'Kelley was to cook the dinner. He had a big chunk of beef to boil and he told us he would give us a big dinner—would give us some "drap" dumplings; so we became very curious to know what "drap" dumplings were. No doubt they were "drap" dumplings, because they went to the bottom of the kettle and stayed there until we fished them out.' We put in the day there. Returning, my brother took me on his horse and some of the others rode in the wagon. We had riding mares and they had colts. When we came to the Walla Walla River the colts began floating downstream and we had an awful time, but I hung on. I had on an old sunbonnet, but I lost it. We finally got safely home.

The summer of '46 the Doctor went down into the Willamette valley and while he was down there my sister and I drove the cows off in the morning to pasture and while we were roaming along we looked for different kinds of herbs that the Indians eat; we got hold of something and started to eat it. I told sister it was poison, but she said if the Indians could eat it, it was all right. I ate some of it, became very ill, but managed to get home, falling just outside the door. They carried me in and found I had been eating wild parsnip and was very sick. Life was despaired of and Mrs. Whitman sent a messenger to the Willamette valley to bring the Doctor home. He came on horseback as fast as he could, finding me somewhat better. I was able to go around the house, feebly. Everyone was eager to see the Doctor, but he hardly looked to the right or left, coming quickly to me, took me up in his arms and then went out and gave them all a greeting. He seemed to be so anxious about me. I always remember that.

Once in a while we would have a picnic. Mrs. Whitman would fix up some food and we would go picnicking in the woods and do different things to employ our time. It was a lonesome place away back there, shut in the hills.

In the spring of '46 we hitched up the wagon and thought we would go with Mrs. Spalding and one of the Walker boys on a trip. We went where the city of Walla Walla now stands. There were just four lone cabins there; they had large fireplaces and big stick chimneys. We only took provisions for the day. We turned the oxen out to graze and when we were ready to go home they could not be found. My brother went to look for them, but being unable to find them, we had to stay there all night. We had a few blankets, for we always took some with us even on a short trip. When it came time to go to bed we had our prayers. Mrs. Whitman had taught us to memorize Scripture and the children took turns in repeating the verses, "Let not your hearts be troubled." We had songs and prayers and then laid down and went to sleep. The next day we found a large fish in the creek and we had some of it for dinner. My brother came and took us home and we called what is now known as Walla Walla, the "Log City."

Some eight years ago I was in the city of Walla Walla and standing in the door of a drug store, looked down the main street. As I looked down the street where the creek makes a turn and where there are many bushes of alder and willow, I saw what I saw in '46. There were some cabins down in there and I said to the proprietor, a friend of mine, "It seems to me it looks familiar."

"Well," he said, "you are right. It is supposed they were put there for trapping and quarters by the Hudson's Bay men, but it is not certain."

In '46 all this Northwest territory was jointly occupied by English and Americans and it was not settled. Dr. Whitman and Mr. Spalding with their wives were the first home seekers to cross the Rockies and it was just a string of Hudson's Bay posts all the way. Aside from the four missionary stations there were no other American settlements, save in the Willamette valley. Vancouver, Washington, was a Hudson's Bay post then.

We used to go to the Indian lodges sometimes. Doctor would talk to them about the Bible and on a few occasions we were invited to a feast where they ate with big horn spoons. Once a year the Indians went to the buffalo hunting grounds and came back with jerked or dried meat which we enjoyed very much. They also gathered huckleberries in the Blue Mountains and we bought and dried large quantities of berries for our own use. The Doctor had quite large fields of corn and the crows were very troublesome; so we children had to go up and down the rows ringing bells to scare them away. That was one of the things that kept us busy. He had a large family and the immigrants came there for supplies. He had to make use of a primitive custom in saving his crops; the grain was harvested by sickles and tramped out by the horses and winnowed. He had a mill out of which came the unbolted flour; we never had white flour. There were some sheep and some beef cattle. Dr. Whitman always sent the immigrants on to the Willamette valley as fast as he could; but many were obliged to remain at the Mission on account of their oxen having given out and he had to feed from fifty to seventy-five persons during the winter months. One of the jobs that I disliked in the fall was when he pulled up the white beans and every child was given a tin cup and told to pick up these beans with their hands. Every bean had to be saved.

We also had hogs. We raised a few, but never ate the pork, reserving that for the immigrants. The Doctor furnished them with meat, flour and vegetables through the winter and what work there was to be done they helped with, though there was little to be done at that season of the year; looking after the stock that was turned out and getting up a little firewood was about all that they could do for the Doctor.

I can never forget the Sunday services and the Sunday school held in the Whitman home. The first time I ever heard the song "Come Thou Fount of Every Blessing"; it was sung by an old Baptist believer at the Whitman house.

In the fall of '45 a family named Johnson came, who had a young daughter eighteen or nineteen years of age and Mrs. Whitman hired her to help with the family work; she also studied and the Doctor and his wife taught her all they could. The Doctor also treated her mother, who was paralyzed. This woman's husband would carry his wife in his arms to the evening meetings, place her in a chair and then all would join in "Come Thou Fount of Every Blessing." The daughter, Miss Johnson, instead of going into the valley with her family went to Lapwai and worked for Mrs. Spalding, and was there at the time of the Massacre. Mrs. Whitman used to go to Fort Walla Walla to make little visits. Sometimes she took one child and sometimes another and once she took me. It was a great treat to be allowed to go so far as Fort Walla Walla, right on the Columbia River. When the boats came in sight of the Fort, they were saluted

9

by the firing of a cannon. I was frightened. I had never before heard a cannon and I held on to Mrs. Whitman. She told me to have no fear for they were only firing to salute the boats.

Once they sent me to the river for water and I became badly frightened. I raced to the house and tried to tell how this queer animal acted and how I felt; they thought it was some wild animal and my brother went down with his gun, to find it was only a huge toad. Mrs. Whitman taught us the love of flowers. We each had a flower garden, which we had to weed and care for. She had my brothers take a tin case and gather flowers as they would ride over the country and on their return would press them. She taught us a great deal about things of that kind and instilled in us a love of the beautiful. That kept our minds busy and cultivated a feeling of reverence for Nature.

An artist named Kane was sent out by the English government.

This was Paul Kane (1810–1871), an Irish-born Canadian painter. It was mid-July of 1847 when he visited the Whitmans and Marcus Whitman took him to visit the very Indians later involved in the killings. The same year that he was at the Whitman Mission, he painted Mount St. Helens in eruption at night.—Ed. 2017

He took pictures of the Mission. We children were cleaning up the yard and varying labor by trying to balance the rake on our fingers. Mrs. Whitman reproved us, saying she did not want that in the picture. It was customary to ask individuals what church denomination they belonged to and one day we discovered a man sitting outside the kitchen door; sister Elizabeth asked him about his church. He said he was a Methodist. She came in and told us, "There's a Methodist out there." As we had never seen a Methodist, we looked at him in wonder; but soon found he was not different from other men, and making up our minds he was not dangerous, went and talked with him.

One year Mrs. Whitman took a trip to visit the Eels and Walker Mission, taking my sister with her that time. She tried to take us on these little trips to break the monotony and let us see something besides our home life. We didn't have any shoes in those days—we went barefooted. In the winter we had moccasins, but they were not

10

much protection. Shoes were not to be had in that part of the world. Our dresses for winter were made of what was called "baize-cloth," purchased from the Hudson's Bay Company. For summer, our dresses were made of a material much resembling the hickory shirting so much used at that time. We did not have a very big assortment of clothing; and we wore sunbonnets. Wash-day was a great day; it meant a very early rising, though the boys did most of the washing. When it came ironing day, all the youngsters had to iron. Mrs. Whitman taught us according to our years, to do all kinds of housework. We used to hire the Indians to dig our potatoes. They dug them with camas sticks. They were good at stealing the best of them, and good at stealing other people's water melons.

I can see in memory that there was a great deal of wild rye grass on the surrounding plains. Waillatpu means "rye grass." Droves of Indian horses would come through there. The grass was so tall I could just see their manes and tails. The land is now under cultivation. The wolves were very plentiful and one winter—'45-6— they became so poor and starved they would come right up to the door hunting for food. The Walla Walla River froze over, so that holes had to be cut in the ice for the sheep to obtain water. Some of the sheep fell in. One day we came down from the school for our dinner and in the kitchen the Doctor had five sheep, warming them up. He had rescued them from the water, but Mrs. Whitman was very indignant that he had turned the kitchen into a sheep pen.

In November of 1847 many immigrants had gathered at the Mission, intending to winter there. Measles had broken out among them and many of the Indians had also become victims of this disease and the Doctor was very busy attending them all. On the 27th of the month, Mr. Spalding, who had come to the Whitman mission on business, went with Dr. Whitman to visit the sick at Umatilla and to remain overnight. The Doctor was very worried because there were so many sick at his Mission, having ten of his own family down and Mrs. Whitman much alarmed about the children. Some of them were very low—especially my sister Louise and Helen Marr Meek. Leaving Mr. Spalding at Umatilla, the Doctor started for home, meeting Frank Sager on the way, who had been sent by Mrs. Whitman to ask him to return at once because of the critical condition of some of the family. After reaching home, he told the boys to go to bed and he would sit up and look after the sick. So all went upstairs to bed and to sleep, little dreaming of the march of events that would blot out splendidly useful lives on the morrow and leave the girls of the Sager family again without protectors.

THE MASSACRE

The morning of the 29th of November, 1847, was a dark, dreary day. When I came downstairs I went into the kitchen where Dr. Whitman was sitting by the cook-stove broiling steak for breakfast. I went and put my arms around his neck and kissed him and said, "Good morning, father," as we were taught to greet older persons with all politeness; also to say "Good night" to all as we retired. I continued, "I have had such a bad dream and I woke frightened."

He said, "What was it?"

"I dreamed that the Indians killed you and a lot of others."

He replied, "That was a bad dream, but I hope it will not

The rest of the family who were able came to the table and we had breakfast; there was to be an Indian funeral later and the Doctor was to conduct it; so we separated and went to our various employments. Many of our family were sick. Those able to attend school were by brother Frank and myself, the two sons of Mr. Manson, a Hudson's Bay man, who were boarding with the Whitmans for the winter in order to attend the Mission school; Eliza Spalding, daughter of the Rev. H. H. Spalding, having arrived with her father a few days before; David Malin, a half breed. 'Eiza was to remain for the winter. There were eight members of our family not well enough to attend school that morning, and most of the children of the immigrant families wintering there were unable to attend. I can recall only a few of these children besides those of our own family that were at school that morning, it being Monday and the first day of the term. School had not been in session before that, on account of so much sickness.

At nine o'clock we went to the schoolroom. Mr. Sanders was the teacher. Joe Stansfield went out that morning to drive in a beef animal from the range to be killed and brother Frank was the one to shoot it down. That made him late for school and when he came in school had been in session perhaps half an hour. When the hour for the forenoon recess had come, the girls had theirs first and we went over to the Doctor's kitchen. My brother John, who was just recovering from a severe case of measles, was sitting there with a skein of brown twine around his knees, winding it into a ball for there were brooms to be made soon. We all got a drink of water. John asked me to bring him some and after he had drank, said, "Won't you hold the twine for me?"

I replied, "'Tis only recess, but I will hold it at noon." The bell called us then, so we returned to the schoolroom and the boys were given their recess. The beef was being dressed in the meadow grass, northeast and not far from the school house. Three or four white men were at work and a lot of Indians were gathered around with their blankets closely wrapped about them and it is supposed that they had their guns and tomahawks under them. The boys went to where the beef was being dressed; in a short time we heard guns and the boys came running in and said the Indians were killing the men at the beef. Mr. Sanders opened the door and we looked out. We saw Mr. Rogers run from the river to the Mission house and Mr. Kimball running with his sleeves rolled up and his arms all bloody; he ran around the end of the house to the east door and Mrs. Whitman let him in. Mr. Hoffman was fighting with an Indian, swinging an ax; he was at the beef. Mr. Sanders ran down the steps, probably thinking of his family, but was seized by two Indians; he broke away from them and started for the immigrant house where his family were. One Indian on horseback and two on foot ran after him and overtook him just as he reached the fence to cross it; they killed him and cut his head off and the next day I saw him lying there with his head severed. Mrs. Whitman stood at a door which had a sash window, looking at the attack on Mr. Sanders. Mr. Rogers came to the door and she let him in; his arm was broken at the wrist.

Mary Ann Bridger was the only eye-witness of the attack on Dr. Whitman and John Sager, which had occurred just before the attack on the men at the beef. She ran out of the kitchen door and around the house and got into the room where Mrs. Whitman and the rest of the family were and cried, "Oh, the Indians are killing father and John!" It seems that after attending the Indian funeral, the Doctor returned to his home, where, soon after, some Indians came into the kitchen and as Dr. Whitman started to go from the living room to

14

the kitchen he said to his wife, "Lock the door after me," which she did. In the course of conversation regarding the condition of the sick Indian, one of those in the kitchen slipped up behind the good man, drew a tomahawk from under his blanket and sank it into the Doctor's skull. Others attacked John Sager. Their dastardly deed accomplished, they left the room, not paying any attention to the fact that the little half-breed girl had run out; then they joined those around the beef and the general attack immediately began. The Doctor was not instantly killed. Mrs. Hays, Mrs. Hall and Mrs. Sanders came running to the Mission house for protection and Mrs. Whitman and Mrs. Hall unbolted the door, went into the kitchen and brought the wounded man into the living room and laid him on the floor, putting a pillow under his head. Mrs. Whitman got a towel and some ashes from the stove and tried to staunch the blood. He lingered but a short time, for the blow of his treacherous adversary had been sure and deadly. Mrs. Whitman went to the sash door and looked out to see what had become of those around the beef. She stood there watching, when Frank Iskalome, a full blooded Indian, shot her in the left breast, through the glass. Sister Elizabeth was standing beside her and heard her exclaim, "I am wounded; hold me tight." The women took hold of her and placed her in a chair; then she began to pray that "God would save her children that soon were to be orphaned and that her dear mother would be given strength to bear the news of her death."

Finally Mr. Rogers suggested that they all go upstairs for safety. The only weapon of defense they had was an old, broken gun; but when the Indian would start to come up, as they did after a time, someone of them would point it over the stairs, and the Indians were afraid to face it. Miss Bewley and her brother had stayed behind their family, to winter at the Mission. She was sick and the Doctor thought he could treat and help her; she would not consent to remain unless her brother staid also; he was lying in bed in a little room off the kitchen, very sick with measles, during the attack upon the Doctor and John, but the Indians paid no attention to him at that time. Miss Bewley was supposed to assist with the housework and to teach the girls some fancy work—knitting, tatting, etc.—the few kinds of such work as was done in that day. The Doctor had been asked to go up to see her that morning, as she was reported to be in a very excited state. He found her weeping bitterly, but she would give him no reason as to why she cried so hard. He came down and asked Mrs. Whitman to go up and see if she could not comfort her. This was early Monday morning. Another incident that fixes the day and time as the Monday forenoon recess is this. One of the fixed rules of the Doctor's was the hour of the day we took our baths, both summer and winter—eleven o'clock in the morning; and as we did not get our usual baths on the Saturday previous on account of the sickness of so many of the children, Mrs. Whitman was bathing a part of them this Monday morning. Some were out of the tub and dressed; one was in the tub and some were dressing. Elizabeth said that mother came and told them, in a calm tone of voice, to dress quickly and then she helped the one who was in the tub to get out and assisted her to dress. This is the hour that is fixed in my mind beyond a doubt, as the hour of the massacre, regardless of the statement of others that it was two or three o'clock in the afternoon.

Now to return to the schoolroom. My brother Frank came in with the other boys and shut the door, saying, "We must hide." So we climbed to a loft that was above a part of the schoolroom and was sometimes used as the teacher's bedroom. It did not extend to the ceiling, but was so arranged that it left a hall on the south side of the building where there were two windows giving light to the main room. There was a fireplace in the schoolroom. In order to get up to the loft, we had to set a table under the opening and pile books on it; one of the boys got up first and then we girls stepped on the books and the boy above managed to pull us up, until finally all were up and hidden among the rubbish that had accumulated there. Frank told us all to ask God to save us and I can see him now, after all the years that have passed, as he kneeled and prayed for God to spare us. It seemed as though we had been there a long time, when the door was opened and Joe Lewis and several Indians came into the schoolroom and called "Frank." As they got no answer, he called the Manson boys and they answered. Lewis then said for all to come down and the two Mansons, about 16 and 17 years of age, and David Malin, 6 or 7 years, went among the first; then the girls. I was afraid to try to jump to the floor, but Lewis said, "Put your feet over the edge and let go and I will catch you." He failed to do this and I struck the floor hard, hurting my head. When he helped me up I was dazed and when he asked me "Where is Frank?" I replied, "I don't know." Frank remained quiet and it evidently did not occur to anyone to search for him in the loft.

They sent the Hudson Bay boys and the half-breed Indian boy in charge of an Indian to Finlay's lodge and from there they were sent the next day to Fort Walla Walla and were safe there. Later, after the rescue of the survivors, the two Manson boys went down the river from the fort with us; but they would not let the boy David go, claiming him as a Canadian. His father was a Spaniard and his mother a squaw. The last look I had of him was when we rowed away from Fort Walla Walla, leaving him standing on the bank of the river crying as though his heart were breaking.

Lewis said to me, "Where do you want to go?"

I said, "I want to go to the kitchen where John is."

He replied, "John is dead and the rest of them."

I said, "I don't believe it, for he was there when I went down at recess."

But he took my hand and the rest of the children followed, with the Indians bringing up the rear. When we went into the kitchen, the dead body of John lay on the floor and his blood had run and made a stream of dark, congealed crimson. He laid on his back with one arm thrown up and back and the other outstretched and the twine still around his knees. It appeared as if he had been hit and just slipped out of the chair he was sitting on. We children all sat down on the settle that was near the stove. A stove was a luxury in those days; there was one in the living room and in the kitchen, where the children sat in terror, was a Hudson's Bay cook stove of a very small and primitive make; the oven was directly over the firebox and two kettles which were of an oblong shape sat in on the side, something like the drum on the sides of a stove. The kettle of meat had been put on to cook for dinner and was still on the stove. Joe Lewis took a piece out and cut it up, put it on the lid of the kettle and said, "You

17

children haven't had any dinner," 'and passed it to us, but none of us could eat.

The room was full of Indians and they would point their guns at us, saying "Shall we shoot?" and then flourish their tomahawks at our defenseless heads. One of them had on John's straw hat that he had braided from straw cut from wild grass one summer when he was working for the Rev. Spalding. Mrs. Spalding had sewed it for him. The Indian's name was Klokamus. Later, he was one of five hanged at Oregon City in the summer of 1850. The pantry was being plundered by the squaws. In memory, I can hear the rattle of the dried berries on the floor as they emptied the receptacles of them, in order to get the pans and cans to carry away. Joe Lewis went into the living room and must have gone into the parlor where mother had a large wooden chest in which she kept her choice clothing and keepsakes; he came out with five nice, fancy gauze kerchiefs of different colors, made to wear with a medium low-necked dress. He gave them to the Chief and the headmen that were in the room.

In a short time my brother Frank came into the room. He sat down beside me, saying "I came to find you. John is dead and we don't know what has become of the rest of the family; the Indians are going to kill me and what will become of you, my poor, little sister?" Word was finally passed out not to kill any of the children and we were ordered out of the house, so we went and stood in a corner where the "Indian room" made an "L" with the main part of the house; the Indians were very numerous, some of them on horses and most of them armed and painted and they seemed to be waiting for something. Soon out came the immigrant women that had all fled to the Mission house for safety upon the outbreak of the massacre; as they passed us their children went with their mothers, leaving Frank, Eliza Spalding and myself standing there. They were followed by Mr. Rogers and Joe Lewis bearing a settee with the wounded Mrs. Whitman on it, covered up with blankets and Elizabeth close beside it, her arms laden with clothing. When they had gotten out of and a short distance from the house in an open space, Joe Lewis dropped his end of the settee. Mr. Rogers looked up quickly and must have realized what it meant; but he was shot instantly and fell and an Indian tried to ride his horse over him. Elizabeth turned about and ran back into the house. Then an Indian came to Mrs. Whitman and took his whip and beat her over the face and head and then turned the settee over in the mud. She was very weak from loss of blood; my sister Catherine told me and I am convinced that she did not last long after being beaten and thrown face down in the mud, with the blankets and settee on top of her.

An Indian came and stood by Frank and another one took up his stand close by and they talked together earnestly; the first one was a friendly one and he seemed to be pleading with the other to spare Frank's life, but finally the ugly one took hold of my brother and said, "You are a bad boy." Then he shoved him a short distance from my side and an Indian shot him in the breast; he fell and did not struggle and I think he died instantly as he made no movement. The Indians all went away then and the women and children that belonged in the immigrant house were gone and Eliza and I were alone. We seemed to be paralyzed and the horrors we had passed through so numbed our thoughts that we did not seem to think that we could go to the other house, as we had been taught not to go where we had not had permission. It was getting quite dark by this time, in the short November day, and we stood close together, when a friendly Indian came; he was the one that had pleaded for Frank's life and he took us by the hands and led us over to Mrs. Sander's door. She took us in and gave us some supper and one of the other families took Eliza in to give her a place to sleep.

When I had eaten my supper, Miss Bewley asked me if I would go over to the Whitman house to take food to her brother who was lying terribly ill in the little room just off the kitchen. He had seen and heard some of the awful things that had taken place during the day, but had not been molested, probably because the Indians thought him dying anyway. I told her I was afraid to go, as I would have to step over the dead bodies. Mrs. Sanders took me into a bedroom and spread a quilt on the floor and I laid down, but not to sleep until far into the night. Mr. Gillam, the tailor, had been wounded while sitting on his table sewing and had run into this room; he was suffering terribly and begging to be put out of his misery; along towards morning he was given his release from suffering.

We got up very early and ate a scant breakfast, as we knew not what daylight would bring. The Indians would surely ask to be fed as they were then sitting in the early glimmerings of light on Monument hill, chanting the Death song. The wind had blown and whistled so mournfully in the night that it had added to my fear and I never hear the sound of the wind blowing in the winter, but my mind goes back to that terrible night; and it has been 72 years since I heard it wail its requiem around desolated Waiilatpu.

My four sisters and the two half-breed girls, with the wounded Mr. Kimball, were alone in the chamber of the Mission house all night, for they had made no attempt to leave when the others had gone in the afternoon. The children were all ill with measles and two were very ill—sister Louise and Helen Meek. They begged constantly for water, but there was none upstairs; the pitchers of water that were there on Monday morning had had cloths dipped in them to put on Mrs. Whitman's wounds. Mr. Kimball's broken arm pained him excessively and he sat on the floor with his head against a bed until toward morning, when he told Catherine to tear up a sheet and bandage his arm and he would go to the river for water.

Catherine said, "Mother wouldn't want the sheets torn up." "Child, your mother will never need sheets. She is dead," was his answer. He went out in the dim morning light and succeeded in reaching the river, wrapped in the blanket Catherine had put around him, Indian fashion. Meanwhile the Indians had come to the immigrant house and had told us to prepare their breakfast. While they were waiting for their meal, an outcry was made that drew us all to the north door in the Hall's room. I stepped out on the lower step and an Indian with a gun in his hand was on the upper step; we saw the figure of a man with a white blanket around him, walking near the Doctor's house; he was near the corn-crib about half way to the house, when the Indian on the step above me shot, and the man fell. It was Mr. Kimball returning with water for the fevered children. I realize that my statement is different from all the others of the survivors in regard to the killing of Mr. Kimball, but I have a clear remembrance

20

of this tragedy, which time has not dimmed or effaced from my mind. According to some, he hid in the brush till the next day and in working his way to his family was killed as he was crossing the fence by the house. I remember the same day, about noon or later, Joe Stanfield came in and said that a "Boston man" was hiding in the brush. Some of the women wanted to investigate, but Joe said "No, don't." We thought it might be Mr. Hall, as he had gone, as I remember, early in the morning of the massacre to see if he could shoot some ducks on the river. He was never heard from or his body found, so no one knows his fate.

The Osborn family hid under the floor in the Indian room and remained hidden until in the darkness of the night they came out, put a little food together, wrapped a coverlid about Mrs. Osborn and went out into the cold. There were Mr. Osborn and three children in the party. Mrs. Osborn had been confined to the bed and this was the first time she had been out of doors in some days, though that day she had been able to go into Mrs. Whitman's part of the house. They climbed the fence and took the irrigation ditch, as it offered more protection for them, being quite deep with the wild rye grass and buck brush growing thick and tall on the banks; then they got into the main road and went on for some distance, finally hiding for the day; besides Mrs. Osborn was unable to travel further. Their sufferings were terrible, all being thinly clad. At last Mr. Osborn concluded to take the oldest boy and go to the Fort, if possible, leaving his wife and the other children hidden in the bushes. He made his way to Fort Walla Walla, carrying his boy on his back; the boy had nothing with which to cover his head. When Mr. Osborn arrived at the Fort he asked Commander McBaine to take him in and to furnish him horses and food to use in the rescue of his wife and the other children. McBaine refused, saying he "Could not do it."

"I will die at the Fort gates, but I must have help," was Osborn's reply.

In the happy days before these tragic happenings, an artist by the name of Stanley came to the Mission. He had been sent out by the Government for the Smithsonian Institute to take pictures. At the time of the Massacre he was again on his way to visit the Mission. He and his Indian guide intended to go down into the Willamette valley, near Oregon City, to winter. Meeting an Indian woman, she told him everyone was killed at the Mission; he was asked if he was a "Boston man" or a Frenchman and replying that he was a Frenchman, was allowed to proceed unmolested. He reached the Fort in safety and when McBaine refused to let Mr. Osborn have horses, said to the latter, "You can have my horse and what provisions I have," and he also gave him a silk handkerchief to tie on the child's head. Stitkus, an Indian, took his own French chapeau and put it on Mr. Osborn's head. McBaine at last gave an Indian a blanket if he would go with Mr. Osborn and rescue the family; but he instructed him not to bring them to the Fort, but to take them to an Indian village. The mother and children were found with some difficulty, and as they came to the fork in the road on the return, one leading to the Umatilla Indian village where their lives would not have been safe, and the other to the Fort and security, the Indian, disregarding McBaine's explicit directions, refused to take the one to the village and insisted that they proceed to the Fort, The little party did so, and were finally admitted. Their hardships were many, even there; but they remained until such time as we were all ransomed. This is as I remember hearing from sister Catherine as she, later, lived close to the Osborn family in the Willamette valley and she and Mrs. Osborn were together frequently; also from the account sworn to by Mr. Osborn in Gray's History,

Tuesday morning. Miss Bewley made some gruel, hoping to be able to send it over to her sick brother. Chief Tilokaikt came in and she told him of her brother and he was very sympathetic and took a number of us in charge to go over to the Mission house. Some of the party went inside of the fence on the north side, while some took the south side which was the public road. When we were a few yards from the house, we saw Mr. Sander's body lying there; then we heard a cry and saw Catherine and Elizabeth coming, each carrying a sick child in their arms. The women hastened to meet them and helped them to the house, which had sheltered us through the night, Poor Mary Ann Bridger was tottering along by herself. They had to leave Helen Meek alone and we could hear her screaming and begging to be taken also, disregarding Catherine's assurance that she would soon return for her. At last all the sick ones were transferred to the immigrant house, save Mr. Bewley; and Mr. Sales, who was also very ill in the blacksmith shop. Sister Louise died five days after this and Helen Meek a few days after her.

This same morning (Tuesday) we were given muslin to make sheets to wrap the dead in and Wednesday morning Joe Stansfield and the women helped to cover and sew them in these sheets. He had dug a long trench about three feet deep and six feet long; then all the bodies were put in a wagon and hurried to the grave. They were all piled up like dead animals in the wagon bed. A runaway occurred and scattered some of the bodies along the road and they had to be picked up. There was a Catholic father who was visiting the Indians and he went up to the hole where they were burying them and helped. He would take hold of one end of a body and Joe Stansfield hold of the other and they would lay them in this shallow place until all the victims were ranged side by side—Mr. and Mrs. Whitman, then the two Sager boys and Mr. Rogers, and so on, then covered with the earth.

There were two families living about twenty miles away at a sawmill which belonged to Dr. Whitman, Mr. Young had three grown boys and Mr. Smith also had a family, one of whom, Mary Smith, was attending the Mission school. The morning after the massacre the oldest son of the Young family, in entire ignorance of what had occurred, started for the Mission with a load of lumber and to get provisions for the return trip. The Indians killed him two miles from the Mission. His family could not understand why he did not return and became alarmed. They finally sent another son by' another road and he arrived without being attacked, but was informed by Joe Stansfield that his brother had been killed by Indians and had been buried where he fell. This young fellow, finding that we were getting out of flour, remained at Waiilatpu as there was no man to run the grist mill. Mr. Bewley and Mr. Sales became better and were able to sit up and get about a bit. One day Mr. Sales was sitting by the stove and an Indian began talking to him, telling him he was getting stronger and would soon be able to work for the Indians; that they were soon to put out all the women and children and they would all have to work all the time. Mr. Sales replied that he was a good worker and would labor constantly for them if they would only spare his life. It was only a day or two after this that the two men were attacked while on their bed, beaten with clubs and whips and finally killed and their bodies thrown out of doors. Most of the women and children started to run out of doors, but an Indian caught and held me until they had finished the terrible deed.

Miss Bewley was sent for by the chief of the Umatilla and in spite of heartrending protests was obliged to accompany the messenger sent for her.

One morning Joe Stansfield saw wolves at the grave and went up there to find that they were digging into it. He heaped more earth over it, but later, after we had left the place and had been redeemed, soldiers going there found that the wolves had succeeded in desecrating the last resting place of our loved ones. Bones were scattered about and on some of the bare bushes were strands of Mrs. Whitman's beautiful, long, golden hair. They collected the bones and again buried them, heaping the earth high and turning a wagon-box over the grave. For fifty years nothing more was done, to it.

Mr. Spalding came within two miles of the Mission on Wednesday morning, when he met a Catholic father, his Indian interpreter and another Indian. Sending the two Indians ahead, the priest told Mr. Spalding of the massacre, assuring him that all the women, save Mrs. Whitman, and all the children had been spared; that his daughter was alive and that now was his time to escape, as the Indian who had joined him and his interpreter intended to kill him. The father gave him what food he had and Mr. Spalding turned his horse's head towards the Walla Walla river. He followed down the bank of the Walla Walla, traveling by night and hiding by day. For a time he kept his horse, but Indians passed near his hiding place and he had to rub his mount's nose to keep his from neighing and thus betraying him. The horse got away from him finally and he had to travel afoot in the storm. All the subsistence he had was wild rose-hips. After a week's travel he reached the Clearwater, close to where

24

his family was, though he did not know this fact, believing that they also might have been killed. He proceeded very carefully, thinking the Indians hostile, but knowing that if he could make in safety the lodge of an Indian by the name of Luke, he would be safe. He was tired and worn out with travel. At last he was close enough to the lodge to listen to family worship and assured by the knowledge that they still acknowledged the white man's God, knew it would be safe for him to enter; but so exhausted was he that he fell when just inside the door of the tepee and his cap fell off. At first the Indians thought he was a ghost, but when they saw his bald head, they realized he was still in the flesh and then proceeded to feed and care for him. They told him that his family was at Craig's mountain and later they took him back up there. Mrs. Spalding, when she heard of the massacre, called the head men of the tribe and put herself on their mercy and under their protection. They said they would protect her and suggested that they start at once for Craig's home. She said that this was the Sabbath and they must not travel on that day. The Presbyterian Indians never travel on the Sabbath and the brave little woman, reminding them of their religion, knowing at the same time that it might lessen her chances of escape, induced them to postpone starting until the following day, when they took her to Craig's, where she remained until rescued from the Indians. She sent two Indians, Timothy and Grey Eagle, down to the Mission to ask if her captors would not release Eliza Spalding and let them take her to her mother; but they would not listen and refused to give her up. These two Indians came when Helen Meek was dying from the measles. Timothy went in to see her and fell on his knees by the side of her bed, praying in his own language; when he arose, he pointed upward, indicating that the spirit had flown.

When the news of the massacre was taken to Fort Vancouver, Peter Skeen Ogden, the chief factor, declared he must take goods and go to the rescue of the women and children before the volunteers could go up there; he believed that if the Indians thought the volunteers were to attempt a rescue, that they would kill all their prisoners, for they well knew that they deserved punishment for their dastardly deeds. With no prisoners to hamper them, they could perhaps elude any pursuing band of volunteers. Douglass objected, reminding his superior that he would be obliged to use in barter goods belonging to another government than the United States, without knowing if the latter government would reimburse him for them or not. "If the United States will not pay for them, then I will pay for them out of my own pocket, but those unfortunate captives must be rescued at once," said this great-hearted man. He proceeded to Fort Walla Walla and called a council of chiefs and other Indians and finally after some days of discussion, made this treaty with them. They were to deliver the prisoners to him, for which they would receive goods valued at five hundred dollars from the Hudson Bay people; it was stipulated that Mr. Spalding's family and Miss Bewley should all be brought in. During the time of the parley small bands of Indians were constantly passing the Mission, going to and from the place of treaty-making. One party in passing thought to play a joke on those who were guarding us and shot off their guns, making quite a commotion and causing our captors to think that the "Boston men" were at hand. They began to grab up some of the children to kill them; one caught me up and started to thrust a tomahawk into my brains. Just then the Indians outside began laughing and the brutes, on murder bent, concluded the noise was all a joke and did not hurt any of us.

We were directed to cook a supply of food as provision for the trip. Fifty Nez Perce warriors escorted the Spalding family through the hostile country and an Indian brought Miss Bewley to the immigrant house where the rest of us were. They took us down to Fort Walla Walla in ox wagons. Among other things which I remember we left behind was a pair of pigeons the Can-field family had brought with them from Iowa. The cage was set in the window on leaving, the door knocked off, and the pigeons were still sitting in their cage—the last glimpse we had of them. After we had been some time on our way, an Indian woman came out of her lodge and motioned for us to go fast—and we did! It seemed that some of the Indians regretted their bargain and wanted to take us all prisoners again. This woman knew they might soon attempt to do so. I was in the last wagon to arrive. We could see the wagons ahead of us going into the Fort gates when they were opened and it seemed as if ours would never get there; but when the last one came up "pel mel" and we were safe inside, the Indians concluded it was too late to make an attack and capture us again. The day they were to receive the goods promised for our release, we were put into rooms out of sight of the Indians and told to remain there. Of course the Indians were inside the fort grounds that day, and McBain was afraid they might repent the agreement to give us up and try to take us captive again. Mr. Ogden made the speech and delivered the goods and as soon as possible they were gotten away from the Fort. But they would not let the Indian boy go. The Hudson's Bay men claimed him as belonging rightfully to them. "He didn't belong to the Doctor," they said, "but had Indian blood in him." The last I ever saw of him he was standing on the bank of the river crying as though his heart were breaking as his friends floated away from him. He was about six years old. There were three boats that started down the river the day we left the Fort, eight oarsmen to a boat, and we pulled out into the stream pretty fast once we started. Indians were along the bank riding and talking, and it was necessary' to travel fast. At night we landed and camped. It was cold, windy and sandy. Our belongings were left for the settlers to bring down in the spring, though, of course, we children had little to concern ourselves about. Before we left the Mission Mrs. Sanders had told one of the chiefs that the Doctor's children had no clothes—that everything was gone. "No clothes, no blankets, no nothing," so he went over to the other house and brought a comfort and gave that to my oldest sister and gave me a thin quilt and my other sister a blanket or quilt. It was the custom in those days to quilt so fine; I mean, with the stitching very close and usually the quilts were made of two pieces of cloth and a thin layer of cotton batting between. My quilt got afire on our trip down the river and most of it was burned. The chief also got us a few undergarments of Mrs. Whitman's.

Mr. Spalding looked after us on the trip and Mr. Stanley, who went along also, took especial pains to care for us. He would do all he could to make the hardships a little easier to bear, taking pains to wrap us up when in the boat and to see that we got to camp and back to the boat securely. When we got to Vancouver, Mr. Stanley bought some calico to make each of us a dress. I think my portion was five yards and they made me a dress and bonnet out of it after I went to

Mrs. Geiger's. I do not know what we would have done without Mr. Stanley. He was so good and kind to us and Mr. Ogden was very kind, too.

We had to make two portages. Once the men had to take the boats entirely out of the water and carry them around on their shoulders and let them down the steep banks with ropes, while we carried the provisions and such small belongings as we were allowed to take with us. We finally came to Memmaloo's island, which Mr. Stanley told us was the Indian burying ground. It took us about eight days to go down the Columbia river. As we traveled, we came to a place they called St. Helens [near Mount St. Helens], then to another called Linn City and on to Fort Vancouver. We staid over Sunday there and the Spalding family was entertained at the Post by Mr. Ogden and James Douglas and finally we were taken to Portland. Some of the volunteers were on the bank of the Willamette river and the Governor was also standing there as we rowed up. Mr. Ogden went to the Governor, shook hands and said to him, "Here are the prisoners and now I will turn them over to you. I have done all I could." He also asked that we be taken to Oregon City, which was agreed upon and later, done. Some of the volunteers were camped across the river and when they saluted the boats we children thought we were going to be shot. Captain Gilliam, a brother-in-law of the Captain Shaw who was our protector on the plains after our own father and mother had died, rowed across the river and asked which were the Sager children and on our being pointed out to him, shook hands with us. Some of our forlorn party had friends to meet them and Governor Abernathy kept the others until places were found for them,

I remember going to Dr. McLaughlin's house in Oregon City.

Dr. John McLoughlin, born a French-Canadian (Jean-Baptiste McLoughlin, 1784–1857) was a naturalized American, Chief Factor (agent) and Superintendent of the Columbia District of the Hudson's Bay Company at Fort Vancouver from 1824 to 1845. He was later known as the "Father of Oregon." In the late 1840s his general store in Oregon City was famous as the last stop on the Oregon Trail.—Ed. 2017

Mr. Stanley had a room there and was painting portraits and he came to take us down to see his pictures. He wanted to paint my picture, but I was entirely too timid and would not let him. We enjoyed the pictures, however. When we came down stairs Dr. McLaughlin and his son-in-law, Mr. Ray, were in the lower room. As we came down stairs the Doctor, thinking to play a little practical joke, locked the door on us and told us we were prisoners again and, of course, we were frightened almost to death. When he found that he had frightened us, he assured us he was just fooling and let us go. We took everything in earnest and were afraid of white people as well as the Indians. One can hardly realize at this day, in what a tortured state our nerves were.

My father was born in Virginia, had lived in Ohio, then in Indiana. Both father and mother dying on the way to Oregon and the two oldest members of the family then remaining, having been cruelly torn from us by the massacre, we girls had little knowledge of any relatives in the East, save that they lived somewhere in Ohio. Time rolled on. My oldest sister made her home with the Rev. William and Mrs. Roberts until she married. Mr. Roberts was a Methodist minister. His sons, in writing a letter to their grandparents in New Jersey, told of their father and mother taking an orphan girl by the name of Catherine Sager to live with them. An extract of this letter was published in the Advocate and was read by an uncle of mine, who, seeing the name of Catherine Sager and knowing that his brother Henry had a daughter by that name, wrote a letter and addressed it to "Miss Catherine Sager, Somewhere in Oregon." He gave it to a man who was crossing the plains; he carried it some months and finally put it in a post office near Salem, Oregon, and the postmaster gave it to my sister. In that way we found our relatives.

I was with the Spaldings for, I think, four months, and I attended Mrs. Thornton's private school in the Methodist church. Then Mr. Spalding decided to go and live in Forest Grove and the Rev. Mr. Griffin and Mr. Alvin T. Smith came with their ox teams and moved us out.

Miss Mary Johnson came to the Whitmans in '45, wintered there and went to the Spalding's mission in '46 and was there at the time of the massacre and came down the river with us. She came with the Spalding family to Forest Grove when we moved. We were taken to the Smith home until the Spalding family could get a house and settle down.

It was decided, however, that I should go and live with Mr. and Mrs. Geiger, living on a farm adjoining the Smith's. The Geigers were a young married couple without children. Mr. Geiger came on horseback after me the day after we reached the Smiths, but I cried so hard at the prospect of leaving Mary Johnson that he went away without me. A day or so later he came back again and still I would not go, but clung to Mary. It seemed to me she was my only friend. The third time he came, I had to go and all my belongings were tied up in a little bundle. A large bandana handkerchief would have held them all. I rode behind him. His home was a one-room log house with a fireplace to cook by. I took up my life there, lonely and isolated. The nearest neighbor was a mile away. Life was primitive. If the fire was not carefully covered to keep the coals alive, we would have to go to a neighbor's to borrow fire. There were no matches in the country and sometimes I would be sent a mile across the prairie to bring fire on a shovel from the neighbor's. If there were no coals, the flint and steel had to be used and if that was not successful we would have to do without. It was not always possible to obtain dry sticks in order to make the flint and steel serve their purpose. Supplies were to be had only from the Hudson Bay Posts, for people had had to leave most of their things behind in crossing the plains. That summer a baby came to the home of the Geiger's and I had to take care of it and a good deal of the time be nurse and help with the housework. I had been taught to sew and iron and repair my own clothes and must have been a really helpful young person. In the fall of '48 discovery of gold in California made a great change. All were eager to go to the gold mines. Mr. Geiger got the gold fever and moved us away up to his father-in-law's, the Rev. J. Cornwall. This family had moved onto the place in the spring and had just a log cabin to house a large family. They did not raise much of a crop the first year and Mr. Cornwall traveled around and preached over the valley most of the time. That fall he took a band of sheep in the valley and the winter being very hard, a good many of them died and his wife had to card and spin wool, knit socks and sell them to the miners at a dollar a pair in order to help make the living. She knit all the time and a part of my work was to help pull the wool off the dead sheep and wash it and get it ready for her to use. We had to carry water quite a distance from the river, as it seemed that many of the early settlers of Oregon had a great habit of building as far from the river as possible, so we children would have more to do to pack the water and stamp the clothes with our feet. We wintered there and in the spring Mrs. Geiger, baby and I went to their farm thirty-five miles down into the valley to look after some of their belongings, as the Rev. Spalding, who had wintered there, had gone to a house of his own. Mr. Geiger returned unexpectedly from California, went up to get their things left on the Yamhill, and we settled down on the farm and life went on. I didn't attend school that year, for there was no school. The Reverend Eels came down in the spring of 50 to teach private school. I went three months, walking three and a half miles each way. Mr. Geiger paid five dollars for three months' schooling.

There were large herds of Mexican cattle owned in the valley and they would chase everything except someone on horse- back. Everyone owned a few of the domestic cattle with them and they proved very useful, as the tame cattle stood guard until the others were chased away. I was in continual fear of being chased by them. They would lie down to watch you all day and I would skirt along in the bushes, working my way along tremblingly to get out and away to school without their seeing me. If these long-horned Spanish cattle chased a person up a tree they would lie under the tree all day on guard. Wolves chased the cattle, trying to get the little calves. Pigs would have to be bedded right up against the house on account of the coyotes and wolves.

While I was at the Cornwalls in '49, we lived right where the Indians passed by on the trail coming down the valley. The Indians were not on reserves then. When the men folks were gone the women were very afraid of the Indians. They were women of the South, reared with a certain fear of the Negroes, and this fear extended to the Indians. When the Indians were in the vicinity they would have me cover up the fire and if any of the babies needed any attention, I was the one who would have to give it and rake out the coals and make a fire for the baby. We had chickens and had a stick chimney; and in a corner of the chimney was a chicken-roost. One night old Mrs. Cornwall spied what she thought was an Indian looking through the chinking of the log house. I said, "Oh, I think not, I don't hear anything." But they hurried me up to investigate and it was soon found to be the light shining on the old rooster's eyes.

The summer of '50 I attended school, as I have before said, going also the next year for three months to the same place, to the Reverend Eels. Then I did not go anymore until the summer I was thirteen. Mr. Eells moved over near Hillsboro, where the Reverend Griffin had built a school building on his place and had hired Mr. Eells to come over and teach and he lived in a part of Mr. Griffin's house. He called it "Mr. Griffin's select school." I was permitted to go there and work for my board, but did not have to work very hard. Mr. Griffin had lots of cattle and Mr. Eells had one cow; when he was at home he milked it and when he was not the youngsters had to milk. Mrs. Griffin and her children had all their cows to milk. They did not wean the calves, but would turn them all in together and the big calves would have a fine time getting all the milk. One day I was milking the cow and I set the milk pail down in the corner and the old cow got at it and drank all the milk.

I had read of town pumps, but had never seen one until I went there and I did not like the taste of the water in this, but Mr. Griffin said it was Sulphur water. Finally it go so strong of Sulphur he concluded he had better have the well cleaned out; so someone came to clean it out and they found a side of bacon, a skunk, some squirrels and mice. After it was cleaned out, we had no more Sulphur water, but I have never enjoyed the taste of Sulphur water since.

We had a garden. I was very fond of cucumbers and my favorite pastime in summer after supper was to gather cucumbers, get a handful of salt and walk up the lane. When anyone asked about Matilda, someone would reply, "The last I saw of her she was walking up the lane with salt and cucumbers for company."

Some of our pastimes, evenings, were to sit together by the fireplace in Mr. Griffin's home with him as the leader in the story-telling. We would recount incidents in our lives and then make up stories and tell them; roast potatoes in the fire, rake them out with a stick when about half done and each would have a part of the refreshments of half roasted potatoes and salt. Mr. Griffin sent and got what he called a seraphine—a small cabinet organ; it opened up like a piano and was a wonder around there. At about eleven o'clock, when we were all in bed, he would go in where it was kept, open up the organ and give us some music. His favorite hymn was set to the tune of "Balerma," and the words were, "Oh, for a closer walk with God," and he would sing such songs until after midnight. In the morning he never did any work on the place. He had a saddle horse and he rode around. Mrs. Griffin and the children had to do everything. He didn't even plant the potatoes. All the new potatoes we had grew among the old potatoes that were dug and stored for the winter and I used to help Mrs. Griffin get the new potatoes out from among the old ones. I helped her to churn and in many other ways. She thought I was a pretty good girl. Mr. Griffin was very fond of entertaining their company with music. There was a man named Laughlin who once came to spend the night when it was raining. We were sitting by the fireplace. The fire did not burn very well and Mrs. Griffin came in with a little hand bellows and blew up the fire. The old man saw her coming and fancied it must be a dangerous instrument of some kind. It frightened him and he got up and made for the door. He finally saw what it was and came back and sat down. Then Mr. Griffin sat down by his organ and began playing it. That frightened the old gentleman again and in his fright he overturned his chair and got out of the door. He could not understand what was happening. So we had our fun with the organ, Mr. Laughlin and the little bellows.

Mr. Griffin liked to give advice to the young. My chum, Maria Tanner, and I were frequently given the benefit of his wisdom, but child-fashion, did not care to be "preached at."

We would see him coming and would start to evade him. Sometimes we would dodge around the house, but finally he got on to our trick and would meet us and corner us and give us whole lot of advice. He thought it dreadful for young girls to be as frivolous as we were; for he called it frivolous because we went down to the woods and sang songs and laughed. That was one of my sins—to laugh. We would often lie in bed singing and laughing and Mr. Eells would call up for us to be quiet. We would be still until we thought the old man had settled down and then we would start in again. Children were not supposed to be in evidence at all in those days, and I sometimes got double doses of advice and correction. But my school days ended—when I was thirteen.

I went back to the Geiger farm where I washed, did housework, sewed and cared for the children. Sometimes if there had been a good deal of trouble in the church, the man I lived with (Mr. Geiger) would not allow me to go to the Grove to church. But we had a meeting at Mr. Walker's home and Mr. Walker preached. Sometimes in the winter it was so lonely and cold that it would be three or four months until we could go out to church. We looked forward to the camp-meetings in June, We had an old mud oven outside to bake in. The people got together and furnished provisions; some would bring meat, some potatoes and some materials for bread, I went with Mrs. Geiger's folks. One old lady said she went to camp-meetings because she got to see all the old neighbors; and I think they were pretty nearly our only salvation from entire stagnation. Sometimes we would go fifty miles to a camp. One of the tricks of the boys was to shave the tails of the horses; another was to throw tom cats with their tails tied together in the crowd at the mourner's bench. This would stop the praying for awhile.

We always picked berries in the spring and summer. There was not much tame fruit—a few seedling apples. The only way we travelled was on horseback. The first printing press that was brought to Oregon was stored in Mr. Griffin's house. We used to go to the old press and try to sort out the type. Mrs. Griffin had a sister, Rachel Smith; the Griffins arranged a match between her and the Rev. Henry Spalding and she came out from Boston to marry him. We were invited to the wedding, which occurred in a schoolhouse used for a church, and the "infare" was arranged to be held at Mrs. Griffin's the next day. I had never been to a wedding and I had a great desire to go; so I went to the wedding in preference to going to the infare [a reception for a newly married couple], since I had my choice, Mr. Griffin performed the ceremony. Mr. Spalding preached the sermon and Mr. Griffin played the organ and sang. The bride was attired in a white dress and a long, thin scarf with purple stripes in the ends and fringe and she had on a rough straw bonnet. Mrs.

Griffin called it "Rachel's Dunstable bonnet." When they were ready for the ceremony, Mr. Spalding stepped forward and Mrs. Griffin placed her sister by his side, putting Miss Smith's hand in his; they stood there a little while and Mr. Griffin said the words that made them man and wife. That was my first wedding.

My next experience at a wedding was when I was chosen to be the bridesmaid. I was to wear a thin blue dress and I went to the place where the wedding was to occur, carrying my dress. Our dressing room was to stand on the bed with curtains around it. The bride was dressed first and then I dressed myself. We knew of another bride who was coming and we waited to get the white ribbon bows for the bride to wear in her hair and the white ribbons to wear around her wrists. The men were all standing outside the house, as the table was set for dinner—the cooking was done at the fireplace—and there was not room in the small house for them. Finally when the bride was ready the best man came in. His name was John Kane. I discovered he had about half of his coat sleeve ripped out, but in spite of torn coat, the ceremony proceeded and then we sat down and had the wedding dinner. The Rev. Walker performed the ceremony. Among other goodies which we had on the table were glasses of syrup. There was something a little bit white in it and I found that it was pie-dough cut out with a thimble and baked and dropped in it for an ornament. The next day the bride and groom and myself were to take a trip. The best man's sweetheart got very jealous of me because I acted as bridesmaid with her intended husband as best man. Engaged couples at that time were supposed to look only at each other. There were two couples besides the bride and groom, who took a horseback trip to Scroggin's valley; we went about fifteen miles, I should judge, and ate dinner with a brother of the groom. They had not been married very long and were starting in housekeeping. We went on to Mr. Tanner's and spent the night, leaving the bride and groom at his brother's. Our trip covered about fifty miles.

The next thing that came into my life, of any importance, was meeting my first husband. In the fall of '52, Mr. Geiger had two brothers come from Michigan and they spent the winter with him and in the spring went to the mines in Southern Oregon, then on the northern California, where they mined a while and then started a store. There were the two Grieger boys and associated with them were the two Hazlett brothers and Mat Fultz. Someone was always coming down with pack animals to get supplies, as they had to be packed out from Portland or Scotsburg. This summer Everett Geiger came and one of the Hazletts came with him and spent the summer, returning in the fall with supplies. One morning I was sweeping the floor and was around with the children. About ten or eleven o'clock a man came to the door. He had long hair down over his shoulders; he wanted know if this was where Mr. Geiger lived. I was barefooted and not in trim to see visitors, but the stranger said "Everett Geiger would be along the next day; that he had stopped to visit someone and he had come on ahead." They spent the summer there. During the summer, they made up a party—Mr. Geiger and his wife, her sister and myself, and a man by the name of Mr. Blank, made a trip over to Tillamook Bay. We went up to the head of the Yamhill valley that is now the Siletz Reserve. We crossed the mountains on just a thread of a heavily timbered trail and were the second party of women that had crossed the mountains. We were two days going over the mountain to come down into the valley of Tillamook and on down to what is known as Traskville. A man by the name of Trask lived there and made butter and took it to Portland to sell.

Mr. Grieger and Mr. Trask were acquainted. We spent a night and a couple of days there; then went on down and camped on Tillamook Bay and hired a boat to go down the bay to the mouth of the river and I had my first glimpse of the Pacific ocean. That was the first time I ever saw any clams. The gnats were terrible. We spent a few days near the shore and then came back to Yamhill and Mrs. Geiger's father's home. We staid there a few days and then returned to our own home. In the meantime Mr. Everett Geiger had fallen in love with Narcissa Cornwall, Mrs. Geiger's sister. I was promised to marry Mr. Hazlett. The two men went away in October, back to the mines. In February they were to return and we were to be married and go back to Illinois to live. But meantime they changed their minds and concluded they would go into the stock business in the Little Shasta valley. They took up a farm there and didn't come down until May. They bought a lot of stock to drive down, two yokes of oxen and a wagon; the oxen had worked or been driven across the plains.

Even in these early times, the subject of clothes claimed some attention of the feminine mind. When I was about thirteen years old I was very anxious to have a white dress. I had never had one. Mrs. Smith had kept Joe Gale's four children during the winter, while the parents went to California to the mines. He had sent up some white goods, scarfs, shawls and so on, but I wanted a white dress. Mrs. Smith told me if I would come down and do four washings she would let me have everything to make me a dress, so I went to the river to wash and I got the goods for my dress and when I went to board with Mrs. Eells, she made the dress with flowing sleeves and three tucks in the skirt. She made undersleeves, too. The first pair of gloves I ever had I bought from a peddler, paying twenty-five cents for them. I earned most of the money that bought my wedding outfit. The wedding dress was a white one and I trimmed my own wedding bonnet. Mr. Geiger bought my shoes, which were poor leather slippers, with no heels, such as the men wore. I was very much disappointed in my shoes, for they were just like old bedroom slippers. I had my hair braided and wore a big horse-shoe comb. I had white ribbon around my wrists like a cuff. Abigail Walker, my girl chum, came over and helped me dress. The wedding day was the fifth of June and the Rev. Walker performer the ceremony. His family, Mrs. Eells and family and other friends were there. Mr. Walker was a very nervous man and when he preached he would shake like a person with a mild nervous chill. Mrs. Eells said that she could hardly keep from laughing during the ceremony, Mr. Walker's clothing shook so. I had the usual congratulations from the guests and the single men's congratulations was the privilege of kissing the bride. We had the wedding feast. Mrs. Walker came over to make the cake. She was the best cake maker in the neighborhood. She couldn't manage the cake on our stove as well as on her own, so she carried the batter in a bucket, four miles on horseback, baked it her own stove, and brought back a fine wedding cake with green cedar laid on the plate and the cake set on that. The trimmings were cedar boughs, wild roses and honeysuckle.

The next day my husband had to go to Portland on business and we went as far as Hillsboro, where I visited Mrs. Eells until he returned. Then we began to get ready to go to my future home in Shasta valley, traveling with the stock and ox team. Part of the time I rode horseback and part of the time I helped drive the cattle. We went on until we got into the Umpqua valley and it was very warm and the grasshoppers were eating up the whole country; they had eaten all the foliage on the trees. We came to the Cow Creek canyon, but the military road had not been built and we had to travel the old road in the bed of the creek for miles. It was very rough and rugged and the hills were steep. We had traveled one day to put up camp. Next day we started, but in going up a steep hill one of the oxen stopped and trembled and we thought he had got poisoned. We cut up some sliced bacon and he didn't object to eating it and licked his tongue out for more. We gave him some more bacon and still he wouldn't go. Finally we hired another team which got us through the canyon, but we concluded it was only a trick of the old ox, as he had been raised on bacon and that was all he wanted. We came to the Grave Creek hills which were very steep. We camped just as we got to the summit of them and after a rest traveled on; in just two weeks from that time two men were killed in that place by the Indians. We just missed being killed. We traveled on in the Rogue River valley which was not very much settled, save in the lower part. It showed evidence of the conflict between the white men and the Indians by the lonely graves that were scattered along the roadside. We came onto Wagner Creek where Mrs. Harris and other settlers were killed by the Indians in '55. They were harvesting some fine fields of grain as we came through the valley. The towns were all small—they could hardly be seen. There was Waitsburg, where Mr. Wait had a flouring mill, and a large log house; and at the time of the Indian trouble, the people flocked there for safety. In going through the Rogue River valley the Indians came to our wagon and were very inquisitive and even got into the wagon and frightened me; and when the men had to be away I would become very much frightened. One evening when in camp on the bank of the Rogue River, we saw across the stream some soldiers who had some Indians with them. The Indians finally took up their belongings and started across the mountains. The soldiers crossed the river and the bugler rode down to our camp and told us it would be better for us to go up to a nearby farm house; that while he did not apprehend any trouble, we would be safer there. We went up there and found seven men, including a fifteen year old boy. They had a log cabin and very kindly made all the preparation that they could for our safety. The boy was very anxious to kill an Indian, so he put seven bullets down in his muzzle-loader gun and said: "One of those bullets would surely hit an Indian."

So we traveled on to the head of the valley and across the Siskiyou Mountains into California and we camped overnight on the summit of the mountains. Three weeks afterward, three teamsters camped there and were killed by the Indians. We came on down into a rough looking country—a little mining camp we called Cottonwood, where my husband had been mining. We staid there a week, then took our way on south to Willow Creek in Shasta valley, where my husband had a home for us to live in and where he was to follow the stock business. We were there about two months and a half, when the Klamath Lake Indians began to make trouble. We lived close to their trail and we were afraid of being killed and so we put up our belonging and went back to the little mining camp. I never saw the home again. We lived in this Cottonwood district near the Oregon line and raised stock, and my husband put out fruit trees and started raising a garden. In the year '60 he had to be operated on for cancer. We had to go across the Trinity and Scott mountains to Red Bluff, where we took the boat down the Sacramento river. Friends thought he would not live to make the trip. The doctors said his disease was incurable and that he would not live more than three years at best. They operated on him. I had left our ten-months old baby at home. In the June before we went down to San Francisco, our house and belongings were destroyed by fire and we went into a bachelor's house and lived there.

Many amusing incidents occurred during the long winter months in the mining districts of northern California, when the placer miners, waiting for the water to open up, found time hanging heavy on their hands. Isolated as we were, we welcomed anything that would break the monotony of life. One locality in which we lived had always given a Democratic majority and the Republican brethren of course did not take kindly to this. One year they determined to beat the Democrats in the coming election and set about it with considerable vim. As there were several men in town who did not care particularly which ticket they voted, they worked on them. I took in the situation and as all my men folks were Democrats, I decided to have a little fun and help our party at the same time. I, too, worked on those who could be influenced to vote either way. One of these persons was named Davey Crockett and he claimed to be a nephew of the famous Davey Crockett of "Alamo" fame. This Crockett was known as "Dirty Crockett," because it well described his personal appearance. He lived in a "tepee" out in the hills and hunted deer. He always wore a red cap that had the comers tied up to look like horns. He said he could always get the deer, because they would stop to look at his cap long enough for him to get a bead on them. Another of his accomplishments was his ability to catch live skunks. He offered to rid the neighborhood of them if he were paid fifty cents for each one he brought in alive. He was given the job and soon came carrying a live skunk by the tail. He said he caught them by the tail and held them so tight they could not scent him. He collected his fifty cents from two or three persons. He repeated this several times; in fact, so frequent became his appearance with a live skunk that some of the business men became suspicious and upon investigation it was found that he had caught just one skunk and whenever he wanted money he would reappear with the same skunk and collect the bounty. A Welshman, who was a staunch Republican, offered Crockett a fine rooster if he would agree to vote that ticket. To this he readily agreed. When I learned this, I went to him and offered him two dried mink skins that I had, if he would agree to vote the Democratic ticket. These looked better than the rooster, so he transferred his allegiance to the Democratic party. Four or five "floaters" seen with equally good results kept the balance of power on the Democratic side on election day.

The Welshman who had labored so hard to make a Republican of Crockett, gave me a write-up in the paper after election, telling how the Democrats won the day by the aid of skunk-catchers and woodchoppers, but little did I care. We won the day by using his tactics and I had considerable fun with my experience in early day politics.

The winter of '61-61 being very cold, many cattle died and this same Crockett made considerable money skinning the dead animals and selling their hides. One cold and stormy evening, quite a distance from his home, he skinned a large steer that had just died and was still warm. As he could not reach home that night, he rolled himself up in the warm hide. During the night it froze so hard that it was with considerable difficulty that he was able to cut himself out in the morning.

An Irishman named Pat O'Halloran was a prospector and miner, and like most of the early day miners, was fond of a drink now and then. He would frequently sit around the saloons watching the card games until a very late hour, or rather, early morning hour. One dark night he started for home, loaded a little beyond his capacity. Not being able to keep the road, he fell into a prospect hole. The hole was about forty feet deep and Pat went to the bottom. The next morning the ditch-tender going his rounds, heard someone calling and finally located old Pat in the bottom of the prospect hole. He went for help. The men got a windless and bucket and after some effort drew him near the surface. Now Pat was an uncompromising Democrat, and as he approached the top he noticed that a preacher, who was the leading Republican in the neighborhood, was one of his rescuers. He commanded them to lower him again and "go and get some Democrats to haul me out," saying "I don't want that black abolitionist to help me out." So they had to lower him until they could find Democrats enough to pull him out. We were eating breakfast when a man came to get my husband to assist in pulling the Irishman to the surface and he came back laughing heartily at Pat's political stubbornness. The editor of the Democratic paper gave him a life subscription to his paper and Pat lived fifteen years to read it; he then decided he had enjoyed it long enough and suicided.

We had many interesting neighbors, men and women of considerable force of character. In the early days of the gold excitement in southern Oregon and northern California a man and his wife, by the name of Redfield, located a homestead on Cow Creek. They built a house and ran a station where travelers were accommodated with lodging and food. Attacks by Indians were frequent, but they stayed and fought it out with them. In one of these attacks, Mrs. Redfield was severely wounded in the hip, but even this did not dismay them and they staid with their home and continued to fight it out. During the civil war she was a Union sympathizer and he was equally strong on the rebel side. Whenever they would get news of a Union victory, she would give a banquet and invite all their friends to celebrate; when news of a Rebel victory came, he, in turn, would give a banquet and call all the friends together. After the close of the war, he was told that he would not be allowed to vote and that if he attempted to do so, his vote would be challenged. He said, "All right"; but on election day he was at the polls. He had a long muzzle-loading gun and was known to be a sure shot. He folded his ballot and stuck in it the muzzle of "old Betsy" and handed it to the clerk, who took it without protest and no one else challenged his vote.

There was a German citizen named Haserich who was known as "Slam Bang" among the miners, because of his frequent use of those words in describing anything or event. He was the proprietor of a billiard hall and lodging house. Being Republican committeeman one year, he called the boys in and told them that a Mr. Van Dueser, who was the Republican candidate for the Legislature, was coming to make a speech. Knowing that the boys were always playing pranks, he implored them to be "nice" and to listen attentively to what he had to say. They promised to behave, but when the old man escorted the speaker into the hall the night of the meeting, there were about two hundred men there, each with his face blackened and wearing a high paper collar. The meeting proceeded without disturbance, but the speaker was not to get away in peace. The horse he had hired was one that had been trained to stop in front of every saloon and sit on his haunches. This he did as usual and the boys had their fun in assuring the dignified speaker of the evening that his horse wanted a drink before he would pass the saloon.

In early days, dishes were not very plentiful. Most people had only tin dishes and these were hard to get. One man, to avoid the risk of loss, nailed his dishes to the table. When he wanted to wash them he would turn the table on its side, take the broom and some hot water and scrub them well; after rinsing them, he would turn the table back with the dishes thoroughly cleansed.

The Rev. Childs (the abolitionist preacher) took a claim with two young men who were both in their teens and full of pranks. The Reverend often used to tell them of the fine eels he used to have in the East, what good eating they were and how he longed for one again. The boys concluded they would treat him to one for his dinner someday. One day they caught a rattle snake and skinned it. As one of them always prepared the dinner, the snake was cooked and sizzling hot when time for dinner arrived. The frying pan was put on the table, containing what the boys said was a nice fat eel. The minister stuck his fork into a portion and put it on his plate, saying, "This is the toughest eel I ever saw." The boys were a little dubious about allowing him to eat it, for fear it might poison him; so one of them said, "If you had seen the string of rattles on it, you would have thought it was tough." The preacher took the frying pan and snake and threw them into the Klamath River.

Ministers were frequently the victims of the rude wit of the times. One day one drove into town with a team and buggy, saying he was the Reverend Bullock and that he had been told there was no church nor anything of a religious nature in the place; so he had come to try to convert the people and build up a church. He made an appointment to come and conduct services in two weeks. He was there, true to his promise, and most of the people attended the service. When the collection was taken up, they responded liberally.

In time the people tired of his preaching, so a committee was appointed to call upon him and tell him that no one cared to listen to him longer; but he was not to be deterred and when the regular day for service came, he was on hand again to preach. The boys decided they would get rid of him for good. A man by the name of George Horner had collected five hundred pieces of Chinese money. He went to the store keeper who had the only safe in town and told him that he had five hundred dollars which he wanted to deposit in his safe. The old man took it and put it safely away. On the appointed day for church services, George had this money distributed among the boys and they all attended church, well prepared for the collection. The church was full and the minister's face beamed with delight to see so large an audience. There were a few men in the place who had been church members in their Eastern homes. Some had been exhorters in these churches and when the minister was fervently praying, outpourings of the spirit, "God grant it" and "Amens" came from all parts of the church and one could well imagine that they were in one of the old time Methodist revival meetings.

The minister seemed to sense that there was something unusual in the air and hurriedly brought his discourse to a close; but the boys were determined that the collection must not be overlooked, so two of them passed the hat among the congregation and the Chinese money soon filled the hats. The minister closed without the usual benediction and made for the door, where the collection was handed to him. When he saw what it was, he made a hasty retreat to the barn where his team was and ordered it ready. When he got into the buggy, he found that someone had not forgotten to put in a few decks of cards and several bottles of whiskey. He drove away and was not seen again for a number of years.

The town was not to be abandoned by the clergy altogether, however, so another minister came. It always fell to me to entertain the traveling ministers and this one was sent to my house. He told me he saw the need of work in the community and he thought we should have a church. He asked me what I thought of the outlook. I told him about the other minister and his collection and he laughed heartily. He preached that evening and left the next morning. That ended the religious effort in our town for a long time.

The ministers did not have all the mishaps, however. A man named Thomas owned the Eagle grist mall in the Rogue River valley, Oregon. In 1856 he surveyed and built the toll road across the Siskiyou Mountains. He also owned and operated a salt works down the Klamath river. On one of his trips he had in addition to his load of salt a barrel of whisky and a grindstone. It was late in the evening when he reached the Klamath ferry and the ferryman told him not to try to cross Cottonwood creek as it was high and dangerous. The tailings from the placers formed ridges and holes that were dangerous in high water. He cautioned him to stay in a house of his close 10 the crossing until morning, when it would be safe to cross. He replied, "I will cross so quick that my salt won't get wet." Fortunately, he had picked up a traveler on the road and was giving him a lift to his destination. They attempted the crossing of the creek and when they overturned in mid-creek this man succeeded in cutting the horses loose and they all managed to swim ashore. Then they went on to their camp, returning in the morning to see what they had left. The wagon and the grindstone were there buried in the clay, but the salt and whisky had vanished.

The winter of '62 was very severe and all the stock in the whole country perished. Mr. Hazlett owned five hundred head of cattle in the fall and in the spring had about five left. He had to go back in March to be operated on again for cancer. He was quite a while in recovering. I went down in June to see him and he returned with me, but lived only until the next spring. He left me with five children and I had to build a house to shelter them. I traded a cow for some lumber and some of my friends helped me. The house was not finished inside. I used to take in washing, which was the only thing to be done. Goods were very high during the Civil war. The orchard had begun to bear and quite a lot of gooseberries had set on. One year we had three hundred pounds of them. I managed to care for my children and in '67 I married Mr. Fultz, my first husband's partner. We lived there twenty-seven years. I had six daughters.

We at last sold out and came up into Washington to live and settled in the town of Farmington [about 55 miles southeast of Spokane], going into the hotel business. Some of my girls were grown and lived with me. We bought a livery business, then Mr. Fultz started a furniture business and finally took on undertaking. Mr. Fultz lived but a year after coming to Farmington and I was left with four businesses on my hands. All the responsibility rested on me. One daughter died. With the help of the girls, the house was enlarged to three stories. After three years one of the girls married, a year after another, and then another. I had one daughter in California; my youngest was with me. Six years after Mr. Fultz died I married Mr. Delaney. We still had the hotel. Then I became crippled with rheumatism and was given up to die, but finally recovered, though told I would never walk again. I laid helpless and drawn up for five months, with life despaired of; but my children came to me, one from California, one from Lewiston, Idaho, a son and daughter living in the house and another in town. They all did everything possible and cared for me continually. My doctor was faithful and the neighbors were kind to come and do everything they could for me. The Chinaman cook brewed good herbs and steamed by limbs and straightened them out and some of the Coeur d'Alene squaws said they prayed for me. Another friend furnished me a lot of Medical Lake salts, which he thought was good for all ailments. After five months I was carried out in a chair and placed in the sunshine; then came gradually returning strength and little by little, with the aid of crutches, I walked and with continual effort and perseverance I at last recovered the use of my limbs. With my sister, who came to visit me, I went to visit Perrin Whitman, our old friend.

In the spring of 1843, when Dr. Whitman returned to his Mission, be brought with him his nephew, Perrin B. Whitman, a motherless boy of thirteen years. Perrin learned the different Indian languages very readily and at an early date helped the Rev. H. H. Spalding to translate the three gospels into the Nez Perce tongue. He also helped to print them on the first printing press brought to Oregon. In the month of September, 1847, he was sent by his uncle to The Dalles to learn the Wascopean Indian language, as Dr. Whitman had bargained for the Methodist Station at that place and intended to move his family and belongings there the following spring. The Doctor also hired a man named Hindman to go there with his family and take charge of the place, as he had left most of his supplies at that point. Four days after the massacre, an Indian came to the house and told them that another Indian had been at their camp and told them that Dr. Whitman's wife and all the men at the Mission had been killed and the other women and children taken captive. Mr. Hindman was so alarmed for the safety of his family that he hired an Indian with his canoe to take him to Fort Vancouver for help. He had not been gone long when four Cayuse Indians came to the house and wanted Perrin to let them in. With Perrin was Mrs. Hindman, her fourteen-months-old baby and a young girl of sixteen years of age named Mary Warren.

At the approach of the Indians Mrs. Hindman sank into a chair with her babe in her arms. She was speechless and helpless. Perrin stood at the door and talked from the inside. He afterward said that if he ever talked Walla Walla, he did that day. Miss Warren stood at the other door with uplifted ax and vowed she would kill the first Indian who attempted to enter. They tried in every way to induce Perrin to come outside, but he refused to go. They finally left and Perrin said that Miss Warren was the bravest woman he ever knew. She never showed any sign of fear throughout the trying ordeal. He also said that he was satisfied that the Indians came with the intention of killing all of them. In a few days Mr. Hindman returned with help and they moved to Oregon City.

Perrin clerked in Allen McKinley's store during the winter and in the spring went as interpreter with a company of Volunteers to seek out and punish the perpetrators of the massacre. After the Volunteers returned, he married Priscilla Parker, a daughter of Sam Parker of Salem, Oregon, and took up a farm near Salem. He and his family lived there until the United States military authorities went to Fort Lapwai. As they wished to make a treaty with the Indians, they needed an interpreter. The Indians refused to talk until they had Whitman to interpret for them. They were told by the military authorities that they would write for him, but the Indians said, "No. Send a man for him." One day as he was ploughing in his fields a man came and gave him a note, ordering him to come at once to Lapwai to act as interpreter. (He afterwards told me that "this was the only time he was ever taken on a bench warrant.") He put his team in the barn and left at once for Lapwai.

He spent many years among the Nez Perce Indians as government interpreter, teacher and missionary and no one man ever exerted such an influence for good over them as Perrin Whitman. Their confidence in him was unbounded and his word always accepted as the gospel truth. They knew him and loved him and would never sign a treaty or take any important step without his advice.

After an interval of thirty-eight years, during which time I had not seen him, I journeyed to Lewiston by stage for the purpose of paying him and his family a visit. The stage driver was Felix Warren, an old friend of mine. On our way there, Mr. Warren said, "You must stay with my wife and me tonight, for I know as soon as Whitman knows you are in town, we will see no more of you." I said, "Very well." So we went to his house. We had been there only a short time when a lady came in. As we were introduced she said, "Why, you are father's old friend." She went to the door and called her son and told him to run to Grandpa's and "tell him his friend is here." He came over on a run and when he looked at me he said, "Matilda, where did you get your hair dyed?" (My hair had not yet turned grey.)

I replied, "What is the matter with you, that you don't dye yours?" His hair and whiskers were almost white. We went to his house at once. He would not even let me eat supper with my friends, the Warrens. We talked over old times until two o'clock in the morning. Next morning early we continued our reminiscences. My visit will always be a pleasant memory.

When the Northern Pacific railroad was building across the Nez Perce reservation the Indians refused to negotiate until their friend Perrin Whitman was sent for to explain things to them. Again when the Commissioners called for Volunteers to go among the different factions to get their consent to the building of the road, not an Indian offered his services until the Commissioners said, "Of course, you understand that Whitman goes along." Then there were plenty of volunteers. They said of him, "Whitman can ride all day and all night without sleep and he never talks with a crooked tongue." It was a severely hard trip in the storm and sleet that comes in the spring in that country; the roads were rough and the nights cold. Not long after this experience he was stricken with slow paralysis and was confined to his bed most of the time for six years before his death. When Perrin Whitman passed on to his reward, a civilizing influence that helped to make the great Northwest safe for the white man went out. He was all that an honest man should be. As I have said before, sister and I went to visit him after my long and severe illness. A short time after we reached there, a long distance message told me that the town had burned and I had lost everything. Since then I have never been able to do anything, but have been cared for by my children. They have looked after me and I have had a good home and the comforts of life. Once, only, I went back to visit the old California home. Found a few there whom I had known and received a hearty welcome; many had passed over the long trail to the better land. Once I went to Baltimore, Md., to visit my daughter, and on that trip I came to realize the changes that my lifetime had experienced. On the vast plains, where years before my childish eyes had seen vast herds of buffalo roaming at will and where all was Indian territory from the Missouri river to the Rocky Mountains, where the immigrant's wagon had toiled slowly and painfully along, with the menace of privation and death a constant attendant, railroads had thrust their slender bands of steel; large cities had been built and prosperous farms dotted the land. Surely a magician must travel with me, constantly waving a magic wand before my surprised eyes! ,

On the fiftieth anniversary of the Whitman massacre, through the courtesy of the O.W.R. & N.R.R. Co., all the survivors were given transportation to go to the exercises attendant upon the erection of a monument to the memory of Dr. Whitman and his fellow martyrs. When the mound was leveled the workmen, to their surprise, found many bones. These bones were classified by Dr. Bingham and others. I went to the home of Dr. Penrose to assist in identifying them. A skeleton of a foot in a part of a leather boot, we felt sure belonged to Mr. Kimball, as he was the only man at the Mission who wore such boots.

The skull of a white woman was, of course, that of Mrs. Whitman. It showed large eye-sockets. Mrs. Whitman had large light blue eyes. Dr. Whitman had a strong face, his massive chin turning up a little. A man's skull showed two tomahawk cuts. I asked Dr. Penrose to hold the skull, which was in two parts, together; and as I went back in memory and imagined the skull clothed with flesh, I felt it was Dr. Whitman's. Both his and Mrs. Whitman's had been cut in two parts with a saw—an old trick of the Indians upon some victims. The teeth in the skull which I felt was that of Dr. Whitman, were intact and some of the lower black ones were filled with gold. Perrin Whitman had told me that when he had gone with the volunteers to the Mission the spring after the massacre, he had picked up a skull among others which he then claimed was that of his uncle. He said he recognized it by the gold fillings in the back teeth, as when coming west in 1843 he went with his uncle to a dentist in St. Louis, Mo., and that was the first time he ever saw gold-leaf, which was used in his uncle's teeth. It was the first dental work he had ever seen done and he was very much interested and it made a deep impression upon his mind. The skull with the unusually large nose orifice, we felt sure was that of Mr. Hoffman as he was the only man in the settlement having a very large nose. A very thick skull, we felt, resembled Mr. Gillam, the tailor. The skull of an old man, we decided, was that of the miller, Mr. Marsh. The thigh-bone of a boy about fifteen years of age, we were sure belonged to my brother, Frank, as he was the youngest killed. It was considered remarkable that the bones were so well preserved after the lapse of half a century.

In 1916 I attended the reunion of the Oregon Pioneer Society and that of the Indian Volunteers at Portland. A gathering of 1600 persons gathered in the City Auditorium. It was a most interesting meeting to me and kept my mind constantly occupied with past experiences. Perhaps the thing that brought by-gone times most vividly to my mind was the trip for the pioneers up the Columbia Highway in autos furnished by the city. As I looked out across the broad river from the height of the Vista House, dedicated to the pioneers of Oregon, the beautifully finished roadway, with its wonderful curves, solid masonry, gentle grades, faded from before my eyes and again I saw a little party of forlorn and homeless refugees rowing down that same river in the old-fashioned, flat-bottomed bateaux, thankful to be alive, but always hurrying to put more and more miles of water between them and the tragic place called Waiilatpu, The chill of those misty winter days again crept to my heart and I clearly recalled the childish awe that filled my soul as I noticed the girth and height of the forest trees on either side of the murky, greenish water that swept on past them with a strong current, leaving sand-bar after sand-bar a gleam of tawny color against their masses of dark green foliage; and I thought of a moment when we saw a little cluster of five log houses and knew that we could see Portland. Then as I looked toward the magnificent city of today, with its homes, churches, schools, its parks and business places, I felt that I must be waking from a Rip Van Winkle sleep and the magic of the moment almost overcame me. This thought I carried away with me. Surely if the way of the pioneer is hard and beset with dangers, at least the long years bring at last the realization that life, patiently and hopefully lived, brings its own sense of having been part and parcel of the onward move to better things—not for self alone, but for others.

THE END

DISCOVER MORE LOST HISTORY AT BIGBYTEBOOKS.COM

Made in United States
Orlando, FL
22 November 2021

10623438R00036